W. L. Shea

Copyright © 2025 W. L. Shea
All rights reserved.
ISBN: 9798312579604

DEDICATION

To my family and friends. Thank you for being here with me.

CONTENTS

1	Life's Baggage	1
2	Summer's Grace	3
3	Worn Out Eyes	5
4	Life's Hope	7
5	Summer's Respite	9
6	Digital Weaving	11
7	Berlin	13
8	Fleeting Art	15
9	Walking with the Missing (Görlitzer Park)	17
10	Walking Tempelhofer Feld	19
11	The Fringe (Breakfast at Graunback)	21
12	Dangerous Joy	23
13	Shattered	25
14	Winter's Grace	27
15	The Symphony	29
16	Dark Gypsy Eyes	31
17	This Wild Maze	33
18	Morning on the Fringe	35

19	The Healing Caress	37
20	Life's Embrace	39
21	Shared Edges	41
22	Morning's Chill	43
23	Gall's First Breath	45
24	Perfume's Breeze	47
25	Adorkable	49
26	Subtle Power	51
27	Setting the World on Fire	53
28	The Shell	55
29	Sun's Prelude	57
30	Rogue's Rizz	59
31	Candy Stripper	61
32	Year's Breath	63
33	The Greedy Wind	65
34	The Hustle	67
35	Morning's Siren	69
36	Smiling Eyes	71
37	Community	73
38	Unexpected Journey	75
39	The Quiet Scream	77

40	Life's Battle	79
41	I'm Tired	81
42	Lovers' Curves	83
43	Life's Parade	85
44	Trust	87
45	The Stench	89
46	My Path	91
47	The Chase	93
48	Being	95
49	The End	97
50	Sunrise Coat	99

There's a new regular at the coffee shop. She carries the kind of weight you can't put down, the kind you learn to live with. She's living on the fringe. This poem is my first impression of her.

Life's Baggage

In the age where whispers turn to roars,
and time has lost its chains,
she bears the scars,
from life's relentless campaigns.

She walks through the streets she's made,
under skies our ancestors couldn't tame,
with wounds that won't heal,
in a world that won't reveal
its secrets or its aim.

Life's baggage weighs heavy on her back,
like an unwanted souvenir from a war in which she can't attack,
each heartbeat echoing the past,
a mournful, rhythmic hack.

The ghosts of yesterday, they cling and hold,
in this age of stories untold,
yet in the darkness, there's a spark,
a fleeting hope that leaves its mark.

For through the pain, we find our strength,
in every scar, a length of wisdom gained,
we stand on mountains of despair,
and breathe the air that's laced with fear.

In this modern world we roam,
with life's baggage as our home,
we forge ahead, each step a test,
bound by shackles we possess.

But in the end, it's not the weight,
but how we bear it that makes us great,
our trauma shaping who we are,
like a potter's touch on clay.

So let us carry on this dance,
with life's cruel, heavy romance,
for in the end, we'll find our grace,
in every step, a trace of life's embrace.

A kind young woman at a favorite place sat down at my table without a word. I was caught off guard, but pleasantly so. We had a brief, easy conversation, and when she left, I found myself lingering on that moment: her quiet boldness, the way she stepped into my world without hesitation.

Summer's Grace

In a quiet corner of my favorite space,
A young woman, her smile a summer's chase,
Sat down with me, an act so bold,
Bringing memories of summers young and old.

Her presence, like a warm breeze in May,
Whispered tales of love in a sunlit bay.
The dance of youth and memories past,
A bittersweet symphony steadfast.

With caring interest, so gentle and kind,
A balm to my heart, a peace to find.
A stranger's glance in a crowded place,
A smile that warmed, an act of grace.

And as she left, as all must part,
I held within my heart, the art,
Of a brief encounter, so divine,
A memory I'll eternally enshrine.

The new regular, the one living on the fringe, caught my attention on this particular day. She seemed different... agitated, unsettled. At the time, I made an unkind assumption about her state of mind. Later I realized her behavior might have been the result of something much worse... an assault.

I hesitated to share this poem because it carries the weight of my misjudgment. But life is messy, and so are the ways we perceive others.

Worn Out Eyes

In the corner of the cafe, where dreams collide,
A woman rests, her life now outside.
Each morning, she arrives with dawn's slow crawl,
In her seat, she dances to the drug's dark call.

Eyes worn by the sun and night's deceit,
She sips on life's bitter, unkind teat.
Dancing the stimulant's waltz, barely hiding the fall,
Of a spirit once whole, now fractured and small.

Her gaze is careful, her eyes always shifting,
Her frame evidence to life's harsh grasp.
Hair dulled, arms guarding her frail core,
A fragile fortress, she's seen so much more.

A testament to life's cruel dream,
In the corner, where the lost gleam.
She hides from the world outside,
Within her solitude, she'll conspicuously reside.

As I got to know the woman on the fringe, I began to see her amazing resilience. She held onto hope with a quiet defiance, refusing to let the weight of her experience crush her spirit. That unwavering light in her, despite everything, inspired this poem.

Life's Hope

In the shadows of life's cruel embrace,
A woman stands, beauty etched on her face,
Each line a testament to the struggle and strife,
Yet hope, like a phoenix, rises with the light.

Her eyes hold stories of pain and sorrow,
Of love lost and promises that have borrowed,
Yet within them, hope's gentle glow,
A strength that the night cannot bestow.

Hope is the fire that refuses to dim,
In the face of life's relentless whim,
A hard strength, a resilient force,
A beacon in an endless course.

She walks through the storm, unsheltered,
With hope as her compass, unfettered,
Her smile, a symbol of defiance,
A light in life's dark alliance.

For some, hope is a difficult thing,
A struggle that stings and does not sing,
Yet in her heart, it finds a home,
A haven, where it can freely roam.

Remember her story, her grace,
For in every life's hard chase,
There's a spark of hope that gleams,
In the most unexpected beams.

It was a brutal day. The kind of heat that wraps around you, squeezes tight, and won't let go. I was dragging myself through it, heading to the Soho House, when a security guard locked onto me and started following. I get it. I've got a bit of a drunken stagger when I walk. But it got me thinking about the ones out there who have no escape, no cold refuge waiting for them. No relief from the heat that clings like a curse.

That's where this poem came from. That, and a bit of heat exhaustion.

Summer's Respite

In the fiery grip of day, where shadows fray,
I wander, lost in the heat's disarray.
The world is bathed in relentless fire,
Each breath a chore, a struggle dire.

Humidity clings, an unwanted friend,
In this realm where endurance must contend.
People laugh behind glass walls,
Oblivious to the struggle that enthralls.

But I find solace in a place I know,
A haven where cool air does flow.
The blessed chill of air-conditioning greets,
As my weary soul retreats.

In this dance with the heat and strife,
I walk, a testament to my struggle rife.
For every stagger, every slurred line,
I seek the strength to let my smile shine.

I met a new regular at the coffee shop. A photographer, skilled with managing a social media presence. Watching her work, I was struck by her precision, the way her fingers moved seamlessly across multiple screens, responding to a constant stream of conversations. It reminded me of a weaver at a loom, swift and deliberate, her machine an extension of her craft. It made me Wonder: are influencers a modern form of performance artists, reviving the age-old practice of audience participation? A play of light, where the watchers shape the show?

This poem is born from those first impressions and the thoughts that followed.

Digital Weaving

In the coffee shop, where dreams intertwine,
There's a woman I've seen, in her digital shrine,
A symphony of screens, a spectacle to behold,
Her world divided, yet her spirit bold.

Her eyes dance, in the hive of noisy whispers,
Sculpting realities, as she stitches and gathers,
The threads of stories, in this woven sphere,
She's the author, and the reader's cheer.

In every stroke, a subtle nuance is found,
As her fingers fly, with grace unbound,
She weaves tales, that ignite our desires,
Guiding us through life's twisted fires.

This artist of the new age, she does not rest,
With every post, she manifests, and is blessed,
In this realm of illusion and truth combined,
She's the dreamer, and the dream we find.

I never expected interest in my book to come from Berlin, of all places. So I went to see the city for myself. Here's what I saw, felt, and breathed in the first 48 hours. The title may surprise you...

Berlin

In the graffiti's dance on the city's walls,
Bright urban decay; a movement that calls.
An art form rich with hope in every artful trace,
The city's vibrant mold, taking every space.

In piss-soaked soil, flowers bloom in parks so grand,
Fountains whispering tales of history's demand.
Bottle collectors navigate through early dawn,
Earning life's small change, a meal to be drawn.

Under neon whispers, secrets intertwine,
As Berlin pulses with a rhythm rich and divine.
Scents of the world mixing; an intimate sigh,
In every corner, her spirit touches the sky.

Berlin, a paradox in both time and space,
Human resilience etched on every face.
Within this ancient heart, amidst the fray,
Lies the hard beauty of the city's unique ballet.

I started this one night, holed up in my hotel room, drinking too much, chasing thoughts.

Fleeting Art

In the dim glow, where shadows meet,
I toast to fleeting dreams and moments sweet.
A dance with time, in a drunken sway,
Borrowed bliss from tomorrow's fray.

The amber liquid, a lover's touch,
In each gulp, my care's too much.
I steal from the future's treasure trove,
To feel alive, to feel above.

As the night grows old and whiskey flows free,
My thoughts echo in this spree,
Yet, within each drop, a hidden cost,
A future moment I've already lost.

But who cares for tomorrow's sigh,
In the warm glow of whiskey's sky?
I drink to love, to life, to loss,
To the present's fiery trust.

For in each pour, a truth unfolds,
Our hearts in stories, our souls in gold.
Drinking is but a fleeting art,
Borrowing happiness to start.

I took a walk through Görlitzer Park and was struck by the open drug trade... so blatant, so casual. It was the kind of place where being on the fringe makes you a mark. I felt eyes on me, measuring, deciding. Yet just steps away, children laughed, parents strolled, life carried on as if untouched. Two worlds, side by side, pretending not to see each other. Posters hung on lampposts, searching for the missing. Young people swallowed whole by the city.

Walking with the Missing (Görlitzer Park)

The sun beats down on asphalt skin,
As children play, and parents grin,
Yet shadows lurk, in each green bend,
Dealers whispering, "Want some, my friend?"

The dealers, too, have tales to share,
Of dreams lost, and paths that glare,
In the park, they find their home,
Among the found, and those who roam.

So I walk, in this urban tapestry,
Where the lost and found coexist in harmony,
A place where life and loss unite,
In the park, beneath the scorching light.

A missing young man's face I see,
In every dealer's fleeting spree,
And as I pass, I pay my respects,
To those who've known life's harsh aspects.

For in this space, we all belong,
The found and missing, right and wrong,
We dance in the sun's warm glow,
In the park where life does ebb and flow.

Tempelhofer Feld is an old airport, turned into a city park... one of the largest in Europe, if I remember right. It's a tranquil place (at least when I was there). This park is under constant threat of destruction, to be turned into housing, which means it's inevitable... If you can, I recommend experiencing it before it's gone.

Walking Tempelhofer Feld

My ponderous steps echo through a quiet Friday morning.
Joggers, slowed by the scale, weave narratives into the landscape.

Where strife and desolation once reigned, lovers now stroll,
Their laughter soft against ancient brick crowned with razor wire—
A past that refuses silence, yet no longer dominates.

The only struggle left is personal,
As joggers chase their elusive best,
Their rhythmic breaths testifying to a relentless quest for self-improvement.

In this urban prairie, nature reclaims her throne,
Ravens rule, feasting, playing, copulating—
Unapologetic vitality against the steel and concrete,
A reminder of life's relentless cycle.

Crisscrossing paths of this airfield-turned-park, history's weight is palpable,
Not a burden but a testament to resilience.
Old buildings stand watch, silent stories etched in every brick and stone,
Casting shadows over tranquil spaces.

In Berlin, the fringe is a state of mind,
And here, amidst Tempelhofer Feld's echoes, respite is found from conformity's specter.
The city, gritty and glorious,
Embraces the outsider, offers sanctuary to those who dream beyond the ordinary.

As the sun rises, casting a golden light,
This walk through Tempelhofer Feld becomes a journey into Berlin's heart—
Where history and hope, love and loss coexist.
To me, this is Berlin.
In its embrace, one finds not just a place,
But a reflection of the human condition.

On my last day in Berlin, I wandered into a neighborhood, letting the streets guide me. I stopped at a café called Graunback. The experience was... less than welcoming. A gruff exchange, a curt glance... small things, but they lingered. As I walked away, I thought about that shopkeeper and myself. How different we were. How alike. Worlds apart, yet standing in the same moment, breathing the same air.

The Fringe (Breakfast at Graunback)

In a land where shadows flicker and fade,
Where strangers dance to tunes they've made,
I tread, a soul disfigured yet proud,
In a world where silence screams loud.

Pushed to the fringe, a ghost in their dreams,
I navigate life's relentless streams,
Hearing whispers that I don't belong,
Yet moving forward, limping, but strong.

Their smiles are gentle, laced with a sigh,
A bittersweet courtesy that passes by,
While the shops close their doors and stare,
At a story that's foreign, a burden to bear.

An irritant, a fleeting scar,
A reminder of worlds apart by far,
They see a discomforting sight,
A truth of life they'd rather slight.

But as I walk through city and street,
Through foreign paths beneath my feet,
I start to see the layers unfold,
In hearts wary, in faces grown old.

I bear the weight of their distant gaze,
Yet in their silence, I find a phase—
It's neither fault nor choice alone,
Just the clash of worlds neither has known.

I stay on the fringe, a stranger still,
Finding solace in strength of will,
Though I'm not wanted, my voice finds ground,
In echoes of a land where I'm unbound.

I met a woman in the midst of struggle, surrounded by the quiet strength of her family. As we talked, I saw something beyond hardship... an untamed beauty, sharp and brilliant, woven with resilience. She carried something rare, something that stirred the air around her.

Dangerous Joy

Her beauty is a dance on the edge of the night,
A summer's gaze with the power to ignite.
Her eyes are deep pools of intelligence and fire,
In them, a storm brews, a torrent of desire.

Wit, sharp as a knife, yet gentle as a breeze,
It can cut deep, or bring solace, with ease.
Her laughter, like the ring of silver bells,
In her presence, all else falls.

Born from a family, formidable and fair,
She carries their spirit without a care.
Ancestral strength in her every curve and line,
In her, all of their essence, intertwine.

A joy, dangerous and wild beneath the surface,
In her heart, it stirs; in her presence, it surges,
It's a force that can never be tamed,
In her, desire is framed.

Since my injury, people keep telling me how strong I must be, how miraculous my survival is, how lucky I am. But today, in the quiet, with no one watching, I sat with my thoughts and faced the truth. I'm not strong. I'm not brave. I'm just human.

We all have a choice when life shatters us... to let go or to reclaim ourselves, piece by piece. Five years ago, I made that choice. I clung to the one thing no injury, no tragedy, could take from me; the simple, stubborn act of being human.

Shattered

To be human is to walk on shattered glass,
Barefoot, yet feeling the warmth of sunlit roads,
To taste the salt of tears and still find sweetness,
In the small, stubborn blossoms growing through the cracks.

Joy comes like a thief,
In the hollow night after the storm has passed,
When the body is weary and the soul ragged,
And yet, laughter spills like wine from a broken cup.

Pleasure dances in the fringes of pain,
A flicker of warmth in the cold,
A whispered promise, tender and cruel,
That the heart can still beat in the midst of ache.

Forgiveness is a ghost,
Lingering in the shadows of shattered trust,
It wears the face of hope,
But speaks with a voice of its own.

To give up humanity is to close your eyes,
To the fragile beauty of your bruised world,
But even in the darkest corner,
A spark remains, unseen, unextinguished.

Humanity is a stubborn flame,
It can be dimmed, hidden, nearly snuffed out,
But it is always there, waiting,
For a breath of courage to bring it back to life.

As I sat in a familiar corner, writing, I noticed a young woman moving gracefully through the room, preparing for the lunch rush. There was an ease to her beauty, a quiet rhythm in her motions that made me smile. In that moment, I wished for her the same steady happiness I've found. One that lingers, even as the years double and the seasons turn.

Winter's Grace

In summer's glow, where warmth resides,
I ponder paths of my youthful strides.
Warm winter nights, now soft and far,
Echo in shadows where memories are.

From a distance, I admire her grace,
Dark eyes framed by the moon's pale face.
I smile, pondering time's gentle decree,
Each season unfurls with a quiet spree.

I sit in summer's heat, shadows drawn,
Reflecting on past moments, now gone.
Every season holds its steadfast zest,
Youth's warmth now rests in memory's nest.

Adventures, no longer mine to frame,
Belong to those in life's vivid flame.
Excitement for the young, calm for me,
But, in every season, beauty I still see.

A bright late-summer afternoon, the heat pressing down. I take refuge in a familiar place, where the world swirls around me. Eyes closed, I listen, the lunch rush begins its symphony.

The Symphony

My favorite sanctuary hums,
Amidst the cacophony of rush,
As souls intertwine and part ways,
In this dance of life's relentless push.

The air is thick with stories,
Voices round like river stones,
Tumbling, turning in their course,
In the quiet chaos they have grown.

Like autumn leaves they gather,
Beneath the watchful gaze of time,
Only to be scattered anew,
As fleeting as a rhyme's soft chime.

The clink of steel on glass,
A melody so clear and bright,
A toast to life's simple pleasures,
Sparkling in the light.

As suddenly as it began,
The rush retreats like a wave,
Leaving behind the echoes,
Of memories we'll save.

Softly, like the first snow's kiss,
Silence reclaims its throne,
In the aftermath of hunger's fray,
We're left quiet, yet not alone.

With my speech impediment and unsteady stride, even casual connections can be rare. Small talk often slips away before it begins. That's why those who take the time to wade through the slurs and pauses, who truly listen, become something more than just passing acquaintances. This poem is about one of them; a young artist whose beautiful style is a reflection of her heart.

Dark Gypsy Eyes

In my favorite space, where dreams roam free,
There dances a woman, a sight to see,
A black and gold muse, in every sense,
Beneath the summer sun, so intense.

Her rainbow belt, a colorful arc,
A symbol of dreams, not just a spark,
Eyes, dark gypsy pools, filled with tales untold,
In their depths, one's heart could unfold.

Her gentle soul, as soft as a sigh,
Yet, within her spirit lies a dramatic sky,
A flair for the grand, the theatrical gift,
She's a siren in life's endless drift.

With every step, she weaves a rhyme,
In her presence, time loses its prime,
The world bends to her subtle way,
Under her gaze, night becomes day.

I met a young poet who humbled me with his words. His writing held a power I hadn't touched in my own work… a rawness, a beauty that left me shaken. But more than that, there was generosity in his sharing. A reminder that poetry is a conversation from the soul.

This Wild Maze

Upon the cobblestones of life's wild stage,
A poet's soul, roaming wild and uncaged.
In the morning air, our words entwined,
Two spirits yearning for truth to find.

His lines, like whispers from the heart,
Each one a work of art.
In the silence of the written word,
My spirit is gently disturbed.

As we delve into verse and rhyme,
We bridge the chasm of time.
Our souls connect in ink and thought,
In this shared space we're taught.

The world may pass us by,
But in our words, we'll never die.
For in each line, each carefully chosen phrase,
We find meaning in this wild maze.

At 5 a.m., the coffee shop hums with quiet familiarity. The early regulars exchange nods, wrapped in a shared understanding that doesn't need words. I watched them, then thought about the difference between the ones who arrive before dawn and those who trickle in after 8 a.m. Two worlds separated by a few hours, yet speaking entirely different languages.

Morning on the Fringe

In the hush of morning, when the coffee shop whispers,
Shadows dance into life from the cradle of night.
A symphony of survivors stirred by the first breeze of day.
A promise of refuge where misfits and dreamers can feel safe.

In the cool glow of safety's womb,
We find solace from the gloom,
A fleeting moment of belonging,
As the day's chorus starts unfolding.

A smile, a nod, a silent cheer,
We exchange with those who hear,
Our echoes in this transient space,
Bound by threads of time and grace.

But as the sky turns pink, so does the tide,
The sanctuary's peace divide,
Chatter fills the once hushed air,
Our solace lost, we can't compare.

Blessed are we, in shadows' sway,
To have a place, a moment's play,
Where anonymity is grace,
And time moves at a gentle pace.

So we cherish this sacred space,
On the fringe of life's grand race,
For within it, we are free,
In ways the world will never see.

Lately, friends have told me they connect more with the poems that reveal pieces of me, rather than just my observations. I've also been reading the work of three poets whose writing hits with a force mine rarely does. So, I'm experimenting. Pushing myself to find new ways in.

I have no memory of what led to my injury or the moments around it. The early days of recovery are a blur, stitched together with fragments that don't quite fit. In that haze, I didn't even understand the concept of a wife, let alone whether I had one. All I knew was the touch. The gentle, familiar, and full of love touch. It reached through the fog, pulling me toward something like awareness. Close enough that, when the time came, a kind nurse broke the rules to snap me all the way back. But that's a poem for another book.

The Healing Caress

In the realm of shadows cast by forgotten trees,
A soul adrift, a ship on unknown seas.
I gazed upon the mirror's icy glare,
A stranger staring back, devoid of care.

The world was strange, both vast and small,
A labyrinth where I had lost it all.
No name to claim, no memories near,
Just loving words whispered in my ear.

That unwavering love, a beacon so bright,
Guiding me through the darkest night.
I stumbled forward, heart ablaze,
In that wilderness of forgotten days.

With each slow step, I carved a new way,
Clawing back memories, refusing to stay.
With each sunrise, a new day of pain,
Journeying through a strange past's disdain.

Now, a story penned in love's bright hue,
In a world I've painstakingly built anew.
On different parchment, its timbre less,
Yet phenomenal in its healing caress.

Earlier this week, I sat in a familiar place, surrounded by voices, feeling as though I belonged to the morning itself. There was a quiet comfort in it. A warmth that settled in my bones.

Life's Embrace

In the embrace of voices so warm,
A refuge from life's quiet storm.
The clink of glasses, accidental toasts,
Laughter lingers, and memory coasts.

In this space where echoes merge,
A sanctuary where my soul can surge.
Each corner whispering its tale,
In this haven where hearts prevail.

Adventures may call me to roam,
Yet, in this place, I find a home.
In the arms of that familiar song,
I find a place where I belong,

So here I stay, in this haze of sound,
In a world where joy is found.
For in the echoes of the past,
Lies a solace that will forever last.

Sometimes, giving, whether it's time, money, or emotional support, can do more harm than good when offered without care. Recent experiences reminded me of this hard truth.

Shared Edges

I see her there, living on the fringe,
A woman with eyes that plead and cling.
"Coffee?" she mumbles, lost in her haze,
On the edge of need, a tightrope she braves.

In that moment, I understand,
The abyss that looms at her command.
Hunger, loneliness, addiction, entwined,
These edges we walk, precariously inclined.

A simple "yes" could set it off,
An avalanche of loss, a desperate cough.
We navigate each other's fragile threads,
Aware that on the fringe, one step misled...

One slip, and you're lost in the air,
The edge vanishes, no way to repair.
Here, where hope and despair intertwine,
We dance on edges, teetering blind.

So, I walk on, giving a quiet prayer,
For her fight under the sun's burning glare.
Knowing my "no" might give her another day,
This side of the edge, where she may survive.

Early fall brought a cold. Nothing serious, just enough to make the days drag and the nights restless. One morning, wrapped in blankets and self-pity, I watched the sun rise.

Morning's Chill

My head is heavy, breaths are few,
Wrapped in blankets, feeling blue.
A sneeze, a cough, a weary sigh,
Yet through the window, colors vie.

The sun begins its slow ascent,
A golden glow, the night has spent.
Through watery eyes, I watch it rise,
A masterpiece across the skies.

Though shivers run along my spine,
And aches make every moment pine,
The dawn unfolds in hues so bright,
A silent promise, life's delight.

In this quiet, fevered state,
I find a peace that cannot wait.
For even with this cold's embrace,
The sunrise brings a touch of grace.

This morning, in one of my favorite places, the staff pulled open the sliding glass walls, letting the crisp breath of early fall sweep through. The space filled with its quiet hush, a cool embrace after the weight of summer. For a moment, everything was still... just the breeze, the light, and the calm of a season beginning to shift.

Fall's First Breath

The summer sun, it slowly yields,
A cooling breeze, a subtle shield.
Curtains dance, a billowing glow,
A whisper of time's relentless flow.

Summer's life now softly wanes,
The earth prepares for fall's remains.
Spring's wild passion, now subdued,
Fall's quiet joy, a tranquil mood.

Holidays, family, and love so dear,
A favorite space, an annual cheer.
My memories wander, a kite in flight,
Life's relentless cycle, a natural rite.

The autumn whispers, a gentle breeze,
Nature's cycle, a soothing ease.
In death there's life, in rest we'll rise,
The annual dance, nature's wise.

On the first Friday of ACL, I was having brunch. The fall breeze billowed the curtains, carrying the hum of anticipation… the festival was about to begin. And then, faint but unmistakable, a familiar perfume drifted past. It was the scent of my first serious love.

Perfume's Breeze

Sliding doors open; a festival's breeze,
I lounge and sip, memories at ease.
A ghost of perfume, a subtle trace,
Stirring the heart, a lover's face.

A ghostly fragrance, a whisper in my ear,
Stirs within me, a memory so dear.
A long-lost love, a forgotten treasure,
Resides now in this scent's gentle pleasure.

I sit, watching sunbeams, a sparkle in my eye,
As the perfume carries memories that sigh.
A first love, intense and true,
In the breeze, their essence is renewed.

The past, ever so slightly, comes alive,
A bittersweet joy, to tease and thrive.
I smile, for the road has been so very kind,
Bringing me here, a poet's way to find.

One morning, I saw a woman who worked at a place I often visited. She always made me smile, but that day was different. She let her guard down just a little, and in that brief moment, I glimpsed someone not just kind and capable, but powerful. Someone with the heart and the mind to change the world. I hope she's out there doing just that.

Adorkable

I saw a vision of kindness and delight,
With an air that soothes my faltering sight.
An earthly beauty, a sight to behold,
A spirit that captivates, a heart so bold.

She sees meaning where others dare not glance,
Finding magic in life's mundane dance.
She pushes her glasses with a smile divine,
Her eyes sparkle with mirth, shining so kind.

Her intellect shines, a beacon so bright,
A curious mind, she explores with might.
Living a fearless life, true to her heart,
A caring spirit, weaving her own unique art.

She finds light in small things, colors in gray,
And brings life to the quietest parts of the day.
May she always find joy, love, and wonder,
In a life that cherishes her beautiful thunder.

My wife always knew how much I loved roasting seasonal vegetables every fall… maybe a little too much for her taste. But now, she's the one filling the house with that warm, familiar aroma. The first time it happened, the scent wrapped around me like a memory, breaking my heart in the gentlest way. Through love. Through joy.

Subtle Power

The home in fall, with its comforts and charms,
The scent of an oven roasting weaves its spell,
A dance of flavors in the air, a tale to tell,
As the oven hums and warmth wraps its arms.

Quiet and warm within, a silent refuge,
Where laughter plays and memories tread,
A time when thoughts gently rest in my head.
Amidst the world's chaotic deluge.

And in the fresh chill of the wind outside,
A symphony of rustling leaves and gentle sighs,
Nature's lullaby beneath the darkening skies,
A moment of stillness, a place to confide.

So I pause and savor this quiet hour,
Embrace the peace, the beauty of the fall,
Where time stands still, in this tranquil thrall,
A meditation on the home's subtle power.

This year, I've met some of the most powerful poets I've read in a long time. Both of them local, both of them hitting like a freight train. Their work made me question my own, made me hesitate before sharing this poem. It felt thin, like it might crumble next to theirs. But hesitation kills more art than failure ever could.

So here it is. After writing this, I realized I'd been holding back, keeping things too neat, too careful. I'm working on changing that.

Setting the World on Fire

I sit here in my worn-out clothes,
Surrounded by elegance and prose.
With creative people all around,
Their words so refined, their talents profound.

I sip my iced tea with a grateful heart,
For finally, fortune has played its part.
But I still feel a bit out of place,
Among such talent, in this refined space.

Yet amidst the beauty, I find my voice,
In the pain and struggle, in the hard choice.
For, I find, within this polished view,
My truth and honesty still ring true.

So here I am, in my ragged attire,
Among the creatives setting the world on fire.
I may not fit the fashion's decree,
But my words are as true as they can be.

The coffee shop finally reopened after a long remodel. The regulars are trickling back in, settling into old routines. The place is waking up again, filling with voices, movement, and the quiet hum of something familiar returning.

The Shell

the sterile embrace
of my favorite haunt
a place where I once found solace
now lies barren, a hollow shell

the ghosts of remodeling's touch
still linger on each surface cold
no worn padded booths to cradle me
in their faded charm, now lost and old

but slowly, the regulars return
strangers creep in, like shadows on the wall
characters too, with stories untold
and the tension starts to ease, like a well-earned breath

my words, going stagnant, start to flow
like a rusty faucet creaking back to life
the coffee's still not quite right
but the taste of it is sweet, like nostalgia's bite

the music trickles out, a faint whisper
of what once was, what could be again
from the back, past grinding and steam
a muffled melody that seeps into my brain

and then, outside, the sun rises slow
behind cloudy skies, in somber hue
like the mood of this place, still finding its way
back to what it once was: a haven for the lost, the found, and me.

It was early morning at the coffee shop, and even the lights felt tired. Rain draped the streets, and the quiet murmur of half-asleep souls filled the room. Then, a young couple walked in. They carried something rare... an energy so bright it lifted the weight from the air. I had to write this one with care. Something that radiant deserves structure.

Sun's Prelude

The morning wind blows cold and grey,
Five in the morning, dawn's official sway.
In the coffee shop, dim lights prevail,
A haven from fall's chill, a temporary sail.

But amidst the shadows, a spark takes flight,
Two young hearts aglow, with joyous delight.
Her coat ablaze, a fiery splash of color bright,
He tall and slender, with steps that dance in light.

Their laughter echoes, whispers filled with glee,
In the corner, I smile4, basking in their spree.
The warmth of strangers' love infects the air,
A moment's truce, beyond the empty chair.

As they depart, the coffee shop's heart slows down,
Leaving behind a gentle echo, a love-filled renown.
We pause, stretch, and nod, as morning takes its place,
The day awakens slow, with whispers of the night's warm space.

The reaction to that CEO's death has been striking. Social media and corporate news seem to exist in separate realities. The gap between them feels wider than ever.

Rogue's Rizz

In vacant lanes of virtue, they align
A common voice, a chorus so divine
"We knew this day would come," they say eyes wide
"A system built on profit's fatal stride"

But in the fringes, where the veil is torn
A different narrative, a sympathetic form
"The CEO's family, victims of circumstance cruel"
A corporate plea for empathy, a plea to be cool

In this divided land, where factions rule
What price is paid for profit's reckless duel?
Can we pivot, toward a brighter light
And forego profits for humanity's true sight?

The questions linger, in darkened rooms
As night descends on cities' broken tunes
Will America awake, from its troubled sleep?
And rise to challenge, its entrenched creep?

For now, the answer lies in murmurs and sighs
A whispering wind that trembles with a nation's compromise.

I met an unusual woman one morning in the park. She had a sharp wit, a wild spirit, and a way of making me smile without trying. We talked for a while. About dogs, about stray cats, about nothing and everything. She assured me she wasn't a stripper, though her name might suggest otherwise. I took her word for it.

Candy Stripper

In the park's gentle morning hush,
I met a woman, a bohemian rush,
A hippie true, with spirit free,
Insisted she wasn't meant to be,
On some risqué stage. She laughed so bright,
And spoke of furry friends that brought delight,
Two dogs by her side, tails held high,
And neighborhood cats, who caught her eye.

Her humor wicked, a spark in the air,
Left me with smiles, and an urge to share,
Memories of her laughter, still echoing near.
I smiled on, walking under a sky more clear.

The last day of 2024 hung in the air, a quiet pause before the clock reset. The whole city seemed to hold its breath, waiting for something, though no one knew what.

Year's Breath

The year exhales its final breath,
A whisper of worn-out dreams.
The city's pulse, a slow sigh,
As if the very streets are tired,
Under the last of the night's stars.

the people, too, their eyes,
gazing into the abyss of time,
their faces, masks of worn stone,
the music, a mournful hum,
a requiem for the passing year.

in the park, the tennis players,
their rackets, a gentle kiss,
the ball, a soft, white sigh,
the bird's scream, a distant cry,
a challenge, a call to arms.

i sit on a stump, a worn throne,
the world, a slow, tranquil dance,
lost in the haze of a fading year,
trying to find the words,
to capture the essence of the end.

The first (almost) freeze of the season came the other day. There's something about walking in a cold wind… it doesn't just brush past you, it lingers, leaves a mark.

The Greedy Wind

The greedy wind is back,
Robbing from those on the fringe.
Cutting deep devoid of care,
Stealing the lives of those without.

The cold blood of the sunrise,
Brings no comfort.
You must find a place,
Where the greedy wind can't find.

Its relentless taking,
Can cause madness.
Unless you can hide,
Or accept it's toll.

Under the pale sky,
I move on with my day.
Taking what warmth I can,
From the rhythm of my feet.

The other morning, I was at the bar, having a late breakfast. As the place filled up, the noise rose with it. Deals being struck, laughter cutting through the air, voices stacking on top of each other. It made me restless. I paid my tab and stepped out, heading north, toward downtown.

I passed the spot where The Kind Man used to sleep. It got me thinking about the two kinds of hustle... the one I had just walked away from and the one I was walking toward. Different stakes, different currencies, but the rhythm felt the same.

The Hustle

Sitting in my favorite bar just before noon,
The space is alive with deals going down.
Laughter over millions lost, as Soul music flows,
And proclamations of friendships bob on the air.

No room for chatting,
Business must be done.
Heads pressed together,
Another day to be won.

My mind drifts to the Kind Man, on the fringe,
I leave the bar, and walk down the hill,
North to downtown Austin, where the hustle is different
More urgent on the fringe, food and drugs are king over cash

Perceived survival is on the line,
In these different world's hustle.
The differences sound the same.
And yet we cling to our separate worlds
like a fool to their fix.

The other morning, just before dawn, I saw a woman rush into a café for a quick coffee. You know how sometimes, when you catch someone in a fleeting, unguarded moment, mid-task, mid-breath, it magnifies something about them? Makes them seem more vivid, more luminous? That's what happened.

Morning's Siren

In the end of night,
When shadows dance alone.
I saw her rush into the cafe,
Like a siren from the dark.

Her beauty was a shock,
A wake-up call to the moring's numb.
Business casual, but not quite ready
For the day's dull tasks.

Her hair a windblown mess,
Strands flying like wild birds.
Her eyes, two bright stars,
Shining with urgent light.

I was caught, a shipwrecked sailor,
On this island of light.
My heart stumbled,
A drumbeat that faltered.

And then she vanished,
Like a ghost in morning air.
Leaving only echoes
Of her beauty lingering.

Some mornings, I cross paths with a woman who is heartbreakingly beautiful. I've tried for months to capture her in words but never could...

Smiling Eyes

I see those smiling eyes—
A warmth cutting through the morning chill.
She stops,
Kind enough to speak to me,
Me—on the fringe,
A ghost clinging to the edges of the world.

There's something heartbreakingly beautiful,
In those smiling eyes,
The way she takes the time to see me,
Unaware of the quiet ruin she leaves behind.

Last night, I was part of something that filled me with warmth... a gathering of people, of energy, of shared moments that linger long after the night ends. It was more than just an event; it was a reminder of how connection can soften the edges of this world. I already look forward to the next time. Grateful to everyone who was there.

Community

The morning after, my body is dragging
Coffee shop haze, the sun not yet come
But in my belly, still the warmth remains
From last night's gathering of kindred souls and pains

We brought our disparate crowds together, a motley crew
From the dive bars to the book clubs, we broke through
The usual silos of self-importance fell away
As we shared our words, our laughter, in a joyous, messy way

I saw the poet with her charismatic dress
And the musician with his guitar's gentle caress
The artist with her paint-splattered grin
We all came together, like scattered pieces of a puzzle within

Our conversations flowed like a meandering stream
As we talked of life, love, and all its schemes
No pretenses, no egos to inflate
Just genuine smiles, and a sense of community that's hard to create

In this chaotic world, where everyone's in a rush
We found solace in each other's presence, like a gentle hush
A reminder that connection is what makes us whole
Not just the noise, but the quiet moments we share, the love we unfold

My coffee's getting cold, but my heart's still aglow
From last night's celebration of life, and all its beauty to show
I'll savor this feeling, like a rich, dark brew
And carry it with me, as I face whatever comes anew.

I started writing a poem about an insecurity of mine, but as I worked through it, the words took on a life of their own. The subject shifted, the meaning deepened. I didn't expect it to end up here, but that's the beauty of writing. This one surprised me.

Unexpected Journey

Life is a cruel bitch.
She cut my throat, and left a hack, a slur.
A stumble in my speech, a stagger in my step.

My quill hasn't changed,
Just the hand that guides it,
Tremors twitching out tales only I can tell.

By the dim light that's now my birthright,
I cobble words together,
Well-schooled in the grit of my own hell.

These nicks, these knocks, they're mine,
My souvenirs of survival.
The story of my life carved for all to see.

Mementos from when Death danced near.
But He fell against my endless determination,
My relentless gasping struggle to keep inhaling.
Keep inhaling.

So, I'll write for those who dare to hear,
The slurred voice from a damaged throat.
A voice hat has been slashed, then repaired.

In the end, though, it won't be about the scars,
Or the way I wade through this world.
Mine is not a tale of a broken, battered man.

Lately, my dreams have been restless... old wounds surfacing without warning. The other night, I woke at 3 a.m., mind racing, body tense. Routine set me right. Writing brought me back.

The Quiet Scream

The sun hasn't risen yet,
And my mind is feeling heavy.
Another night of broken sleep,
Another night of tortured dreams.

I write to bleed, to purge, to scream,
To let the poison out, to let the demons dream.
I write to find my way, to find my voice,
To rise above it all, and make any choice.

For now, this moment is mine,
A sanctuary amidst chaos.
Here, I can breathe, I can think,
Here, I can simply be.

The shadows creep, the ghosts appear,
The weight of the world; the sting of fear.
But still I sit, still I write,
Still I hold on to this fragile light.

A few months ago, I met a woman who struck me instantly. I think she felt something similar, one of the first things she said was that she felt a connection. She's shared some of her writing with me, and it's more powerful than most of what I've written recently. In a way, she changed how I approach my poetry. Her words remind me of my own before my brain injury. But more than her writing, it's her strength that stays with me. She carries something rare, an unshaken, undeniable force of spirit.

Life's Battle

Her eyes tell a story
Of caution, of pain, of a past that won't fade.
Her smile, a warm glow,
Touches her eyes like a whispered secret.

I see a strength in her,
A kindred spirit I recognize.
She saw it in me too,
A shared understanding.

Now I watch as she faces her demons,
With a courage I can only aspire to.
She takes on the wounds of compromise,
Unflinching, a warrior hardened by battle.

Standing firm, armored in love and kindness,
Guarding her heart; a fortress under siege.
She is strength.
Not some macho posturing, but the real thing.

My back was killing me, and my mood wasn't much better.

I'm Tired

The blank screen of my phone,
The face I see, judging me.
Demanding another page of sweat
From my already wrung-out soul.

Damn rain keeps hammering on the window,
A thousand icy fingers stealing the heat.
My back hurts like I slept on concrete,
Feet feel full of lead weights.

The sun is a ghost today,
Behind clouds thick as my pain-ridden thoughts.
This day feels like it weighs 500 pounds,
And it isn't even off the mat yet.

Another espresso might loosen things up.
But right now…
Right now I feel like a broken-down car,
Waiting for the tow truck of oblivion to show up.

On Valentine's Day, I noticed two young lovers sitting close, their heads bent together in quiet intimacy. It made me smile, knowing what the near future likely held for them… the rush of passion, the slow unfolding of comfort, and all the possibilities in between.

Lovers' Curves

The curves of their bodies,
Alluringly wrapped for the other.
Heads bowed together,
Promising nights of pleasure.

Lips smiling,
Glinting eyes.
Soft and hard merging,
Singing nature's song.

Across the cafe, I watch,
The lovers' curves,
Bend into each other,
Whispering passions.

Pleasure's potential crackles,
Glistening in every whisper.
Early echoes of cozy comfort,
Wrapped in the hush of old sweaters.

As I settled into a routine, one seat by the window kept pulling my attention. Every morning, I watched it, noticing the constant rotation of people who sat there. I had written three stanzas about this quiet observation, but the fourth wouldn't come… until one morning.

A regular, someone I'd come to know, was chatting with a customer when things took a turn. The customer started spewing bile, ugly words, and veiled threats. It didn't last long. The regular shut it down, and the coward bolted. The whole scene stuck with me, and that lingering unease found its way into the fourth stanza.

Life's Parade

A man with a well trimmed beard sits,
Where a man lost in a chemical maze was yesterday.
The day before, entrepreneurs schemed,
Before that, a schizophrenic held court.

We're all sharing seats in this coffee shop,
Our lives touching, separated only by time.
Connected by where our asses rest,
And the bitter taste of our shared addiction.

The endless shuffle of the mornings,
Wearing down the cafe's chairs.
A parade of humanity's shared grind,
As we travel from one seat to another.

Our own shit mingles,
With the others'.
Wiped clean with each morning's antiseptic,
But trace memories remain.

I made the mistake of watching the news.

Trust

These men walk through sinkholes
They call boardrooms,
Laughing like car alarms in a dead city.

The TV hums hymns for the hollow,
Silk ties tightening around necks
That never knew sweat,
Unless it was a hooker's.

They trade souls in back alleys,
Palm greased with numbers
That bleed out of paychecks,
And into offshore graves.

You want heroes?
Look at the rats gnawing last week's trash,
At least they don't pretend
It's a five-course meal.

Trust is a dog
That starved in their gated yards.
We're just the shit
They scrape off Italian leather.

Sink a fist into your pocket.
Count the lint, the crumbs.
That's the anthem they left us.
Sing it raw.

After a few conversations with two friends, a more political poem took shape, born from frustration, sharpened by reality.

The Stench

In power suits, they stride with ease,
Their words are smooth, their smiles a breeze.
But behind the scenes, they make their deals,
And line their pockets through corruption.

They speak of justice, of equality too,
But their actions show a different view.
They serve the wealthy, the ones who pay,
And leave the common man broke.

Their lies are lavish, their truths hard to find,
They twist and turn, leaving us all behind.
In a world of chaos, they thrive in the dank,
And laugh at us, all the way to the grave.

So heed my warning, friend, don't be a chump,
Never trust a rich politician.
Don't leave your life's prosperity to chance,
Never trust a rich politician.

The second gathering of artists came and went. Not many showed up. It was good… full of stories, laughter… but it could have been more. Still, I wake up with something left from the night before, something worth holding onto.

My Path

Early morning in the coffee shop,
Steam rises like ghosts in the last breath of night.
Baristas chatter, voices unrestrained,
No customers to impress, just me and my thoughts.

Last night's gathering, sparse but hearty,
Laughter still echoes in my bones.
A decadence of stories and shared delights,
Yet absence lingered, a shadow on our feast.

Resilience brewed in the cups,
Warmth found in coldness.
Unexpected pleasure in the quiet,
Beauty in the reminiscences.

Finding joy where it lingers,
Inspiration when it comes.
In this morning's steam and laughter,
I find a warmth that stays.

A new friend told me about someone struggling with a TBI. It got me thinking about my own struggle… about what kept me moving forward. Laughter helped. At first, just hearing it. Then, eventually, laughing myself. But more than anything, I needed something to hold onto, something I could fix in my mind. For me, it was a three-legged dog. A dog like that doesn't hesitate when life gets harder. The ball is thrown, and nothing else matters. The Chase is on.

The Chase

In the shade of the tree that endures all storms,
A shadow limps, erratic, and broken.
Scarred from countless falls, yet undeterred,
chasing light where the dark still clings.

Each stumble, a strike against the dust,
Gravel biting at raw skin and bone.
The ball: filthy, frayed, spit-soaked,
Glows in the filth, daring all to follow.

No surrender, only the chase,
Where every scrape, every ego's bruise,
Feeds the fire, keeps the breath,
Demands the body move again.

Let the dark winds howl, the rains descend,
This dog knows its purpose is clear.
No choice. Only the chase.
I fall. I bleed. I get up again.

It's been almost a year since I last saw the woman I wrote Life's Baggage about. Now, I've become part of her paranoia. It saddens me, but I am not equipped to help in the way she needs. All I can offer is conversation… simple, unburdened by expectation… she has rejected that.

Being

She lives on the fringe,
Once a friend, now a ghost
Who curses my name between coffee sips.

I wanted to help,
But her mind is a locked room of paranoia.
I've become just another watcher at the door.

Still, I admire her.
Life beats her down,
Takes her home, her husband, her footing,
But she never bows, never begs.

She wears her ruin like a crown.
Unshaken, unrepentant,
Uncompromisingly human.

A friend and I were talking about life, and the conversation led me to a challenge: to put into words what I experienced in my own near-death moment.

The End

I touched death once,
It was neither hot nor cold.
There was no judgement waiting,
No clouds nor flames.

As my body and brain shut down,
I saw the truth in ending.
No soft angel kisses,
Nor harsh demon whips.

It is simple oblivion.
Like turning off the light.
There is nothing waiting after this,
And that's the most comforting thing.

Take it from me, a man who touched death once,
It's a privilege to feel, to exist.
But know I don't fear the peace,
The encompassing lack of being that is The End.

I thought I was done with this book.

Then, one morning, just as the sun was rising, a woman walked into the coffee shop, carrying her daughter. The child's coat was the same salmon-pink as the sky.

As I watched, more women entered with toddlers, and soon the café was filled with small, staggering figures, wide-eyed, clinging, half-dreaming.

Life carries itself forward in the arms of the young.

I had to add these pages last minute, to make the book complete.

The Sunrise Coat

Her smile cracked open the morning,
A child's coat pulled dawn from the sky.
The cafe became an altar of Cheerios,
With spilled apple juice scriptures.

Stroller wheels churning gospel,
Confusion sticky as jam on cheeks.
In that moment we worshipped,
At the shrine of mismatched mittens.

That pink still blisters
Through my concrete afternoon.
Sunrise clawed into denim,
By small relentless hands.

And tomorrow, again, the sun will rise,
Soft hands tugging at the hem of morning.
Another pink dawn, another open door,
The world waking in warm, familiar chaos.

Made in the USA
Columbia, SC
17 March 2025